THE
MODERN DANCE
OF DEATH

THE
MODERN DANCE
OF DEATH

By

PEYTON ROUS

THE
LINACRE LECTURE
1929

CAMBRIDGE
AT THE UNIVERSITY PRESS
MCMXXIX

*The design on the cover
is from Hollar's engraving
of Holbein's painting of*
THE PHYSICIAN (*see p.* 5)

CAMBRIDGE UNIVERSITY PRESS
Cambridge, New York, Melbourne, Madrid, Cape Town,
Singapore, São Paulo, Delhi, Tokyo, Mexico City

Cambridge University Press
The Edinburgh Building, Cambridge CB2 8RU, UK

Published in the United States of America by Cambridge University Press, New York

www.cambridge.org
Information on this title: www.cambridge.org/9781107652927

© Cambridge University Press 1929

First published 1929
First paperback edition 2011

A catalogue record for this publication is available from the British Library

ISBN 978-1-107-65292-7 Paperback

THE
MODERN DANCE OF DEATH

IN the time of Thomas Linacre men had
a passion—strange it now seems to us—
for pictures in which they danced with
Death. Rather was it Death that danced[1].
They were shown as passive, poor things,
seldom raising a hand in deprecation or surprise. Out of them all only the idiot danced,
cutting a lumbering caper as he was hurried
away.

The vogue of these pictures passed in the
sixteenth century. The Protector Somerset
destroyed the Dance of Death in St Paul's
in 1549, when he pulled down the Pardon
Chapel to gain material for his new mansion
in the Strand. The great Dance of Death at
Basel and that in the Cemetery of the Inno-
cents at Paris were let fall into decay. New
Dances ceased to be printed. For men's
mood had changed, not again to be so down-
cast. It is my purpose to discuss whether,
since Linacre's period, the underlying dance
of death has also changed—that visible to

[1] Peignot, G., "La Mort est la coryphée," *Recherches
sur les danses des morts*, Dijon, 1826.

the student of morbid physiology. There is no need to recite again the tale of the increased length of life that we now enjoy, or to name one by one those ills which have been thrust into limbo. My attempt shall be to deal with actions and reactions within the diseased organism. In how far have these been altered since Linacre? He died nearly twenty years before the human body was first accurately described. The sweep of knowledge and of activity that we regard as modern had not begun to gather way in his time.

Much calamitous history of persons great and small and of mental states went to the making of the old Dances of Death. They tell vehemently of the conditions of life. When one compares them with those other picture books bearing the same name which are printed in these present days significant differences are seen. Even in the last and most consummate of the old dances, Holbein's *Imagines Mortis*, the artistry is a mere instrument wherewith to proclaim a rancour at the injustices of the world and a sense of the nearness of swift death. One need not describe so familiar a book. But one may flick its leaves over, pausing here and there. One sees that Death makes a distinction amongst persons and that these are often horridly startled, as not in the other *Danses macabres*. The harsh noble, the cardinal selling benefices, the bribed judge, the paunchy abbot, the counsellor at law who would give no ear to the poor, the lying friar, the nun that was a wanton, the too-rich man,—these Death, roughly or with a leering ingenuity, pulls away. He pours wine for the drunkard, brusquely interrupts the gamester, and seizes the robber in the nick of time. Often he is assisted by little devils, notably as he deals with the Pope; for it was in 1524 that the blocks were cut, with Luther just excommunicated; and Holbein was of Augsburg. The takings off of the good and the poor, who are very often the same persons, though sudden, show in general less bitterness. The family gaze with more of surprise than affright as the child is led briskly out. Always, nearly, the little pictures have an hour-glass somewhere close at hand, perched on chair or under table. The hour could not be disputed. The physician is a mere onlooker as Death struts in with a patient. Nowhere in the scenes is there an attempt to stay Death's hand.

The recent Dances lack this bitterness and this fatalism. For many generations, though there were reprints from time to time, new ones appeared at long intervals only. But of late, notably since the War, not a few have been printed. Even before it they were mostly Teutonic. The English seem always to have been averse to the macabre symbolism, which in Linacre's day found expression on only a few cloister walls. Sir Thomas More had an aversion to the paintings in St Paul's, "ye lothely figure of our dead, bony bodies." The new Dances have most of them no greater meaning than that of a dallying with grisly images. They show Death interrupting the individuals of a highly various, democratic society, or bringing mortals to grief with the aid of modern contrivances or through modern pursuits, aeroplanes, motor cars, mountain-climbing and the like. These are mere tattle at an inquest. Some few are designedly horrors. Only in the series which deal with the War does one find the old fatalism, amongst them the English dance by Percy Smith of Death amidst the wire entanglements. There is a new note for a whole series in Strang's Death as Healer. In connection therewith one recalls the enfolding serenity of Death and the Old Man at Sunset, by Rethel. Occasionally the misery of the poor or of

(4)

the weak is depicted still; but for the most part the ancient reliance on Death as an irresistible leveller is gone. One sees that people know how often his activities can be deferred, that men no longer have such bitterness as would lead them to find satisfaction in his ravages.

These differences in the pictures of Death's achievements can take the place of a thick, antiquarian essay on the differences in the conditions of existence then and now. And yet, since the Dances have stiffened to a convention, they do not declare the changes in full measure. Elsewhere in art one sees them more clearly. In ancient days art dealt with the violent or the obvious; for life was concerned with these. In the bas-relief known as the Palette of Narmer, this king of early Egypt contemplates his enemies who are laid in ranks before him, each man's severed head between his knees. Now the progress in security has brought mankind to a state in which novels, enthralling ones, can be written upon the glints and flashes of thought within the mind of an anaemic, irresolute individual during the course of a single day. Descriptions of manslaughter are no longer a literary necessity and often a gross *faux pas*.

Painting expresses the same progress, and an even greater tolerance. Soon the security (between wars) will have made all so quiet that it will be possible to hear the grass grow—the grass of the intellect—and, what is better, to enjoy the minute vibrations.

The altered conditions of existence have softened the influence of the image of death to affect the body through the mind. We live more than twice as long as did persons in Linacre's time, when to be an old man was well-nigh a profession in itself. Even at the end of the eighteenth century only nine individuals out of the hundred lived to be fifty instead of more than half the number as now happens. And we are freed to an even greater extent than this respite indicates from the dying of deaths in thought before the real one, the lesson no longer standing forth starkly that what is happening to one's neighbour must inevitably come upon oneself. The death of ageing individuals, such as we all at present tend to become, evokes fewer injurious questions amongst people at large than the extinguishing of youth. At first thought it seems extraordinary that the generations who did not nearly live out a natural life should have panted after the elixir for an everlasting one. But the occupation with the idea of impending death was then only too frequently not a preoccupation. Now people are busy living out their newly acquired days—allotted days of which they have been deprived heretofore—and in adjusting themselves to an existence which involves their being born afresh each morning into a more vivid world. There exists a relative contentment with the conception of three score and ten, since it so often becomes actuality and the years are crammed with the unexpected. Were a census to be taken of states of mind one cannot doubt that, save for the scientist, it would show only the ageing to be greatly concerned now with the effort to prolong life. It may be questioned, on the other hand, whether the old are less reluctant to go than the old of Linacre's day, since even for them so much exists to live for. Metschnikoff's announcement at 72 that the dislike for dying which had led him to conceive it unnatural and to strive to defer it, had made way for a welcoming spirit, must be viewed in the light of his physical condition. For it will be recalled that he had a crippled heart and was worn with the struggle to vindicate in his own person his thesis that man should by right live longer. But whatever the state of mind of the old as affecting their bodies— and Sir Humphry Rolleston has told in a preceding lecture how great this influence is[1]—there can be no doubt that, viewed in the searching light of utility, it is less important than that of the young. For the mental states of the old as affecting the body find but short shrift, whereas those of the young a long tether. One would say off-hand that in addition to all other ameliorations in life the turning away of the young from Death's image must have done much to influence our physical actions and reactions.

From the moment that the body becomes a going concern it must fight for its integrity. Its Dance with Death begins long before birth and never ceases throughout the lengthening period of what we call health. Everything coming in contact with it shapes its destiny; and for it there is assuredly no such thing as Free Will. Were the healthy persons of Linacre's time different from those now strolling about?

Perhaps you will allow without a marshalling of truisms that we now live deliciously free of a host of nagging, physical

[1] Rolleston, Sir Humphry, *Some Medical Aspects of Old Age*, Macmillan and Co., Ltd., London, 1922.

(8)

irksomenesses which the healthy masses of the year 1520 carried about as a matter of course. It is all very well to cite, as against this statement, the fact that rickets did not appear in England until after windows had been glazed, with the result that children could stay inside comfortably and unwholesomely. Human beings have an incorrigible habit of testing the sharpness of new implements upon their own persons.

This is a long preamble; but it prepares one to expect large changes in the character of those morbid actions and reactions which threaten life. And yet another reason for such expectation lies in the methods of the modern physician, so much surer in aim and effect than those of the older day. No need to point out that the efforts of the old leech were in general bungling; that many of his draughts and clysters compounded from a picturesque material were but so much sound and fury. The "oyle of whelpes," described as a sovereign balsam for wounds by the matter-of-fact Paré, a generation after Linacre, was merely a bland, sterile emollient achieved by boiling in oil of lilies two new-born puppies together with a pound of earthworms, and skimming the pot. Nevertheless it cannot be said that the treatment of Linacre's time lacked in either decision or the drastic note; and throughout it a pathetic assiduity is visible. But modern treatments have a piercing quality based upon understanding. One must often still inflict injury in order to cure greater evils; and some of the curative injuries now employed are new in type. If it be possible to stop the course of an osteogenic sarcoma by inducing toxaemia with Coley's serum, or to relieve intestinal obstruction by enterostomy, or rheumatism by anaphylactic shock, the modern physician cannot hesitate. But do not these methods introduce a changed pathology? Have not our increasing interventions brought with them unprecedented morbid states?

It will be simplest to begin by scanning, item by item, the International List of Causes of Death. There is scarcely a cause out of the entire 189 against which one cannot write "Less prevalent than in 1500" or "Seen no more" or "Greatly alleviated." There is immensely less pus and no plague in occidental lands. But of few diseases indeed can one put down "Existing still, but with an essentially new pathology." Innumerable quantitative alterations there have been amongst the infections, and quali-

(10)

tative too, in the sense that mild lesions are not the same as severe ones. But the tubercle and the gumma, the typhoid ulcer and the carbuncle remain intrinsically what they were. The varioloid of patients only partially protected by an old vaccination is smallpox still. The cardiovascular or neural syphilis of those insufficiently treated with modern remedies is still morphologically syphilis, though the life of the individuals has been so greatly prolonged as to permit these late phases of the disease to elaborate themselves. The involutionary processes that take place in paretics given tryparsamide are no bizarre manifestations but those of a "natural" healing. So too with those of leprosy after chaulmoogra oil. And though crisis can be induced with anti-serum in pneumonia cases of Group I, the lesions that had come into being run their appointed course. The sequelae to which people succumb who have been enabled to stand the first brunt of a disease, are ordinarily the same as in the past though rarely seen then; and abortive attacks differ from typical ones mainly in the extent and severity of the lesions, not in their intrinsic character. It is true that clean wounds heal nowadays by first intention, and that infected ones can be rendered clean as never before; but healing *per primam* was far from unknown in Linacre's day. The most astonishing and effective of functional exploitations, the purposeful stimulation of the mechanisms which produce immunity, has led to but a negligible new pathology, though it might conceivably, when pushed to hyperimmunization, have engendered lesions as concrete and peculiar as amyloid, injuries only tolerable because of the ill thereby averted, as in the case of the Wortley Montague inoculations against smallpox. Some incidental anaphylaxis there is, but less and less as sera are purified. Allergy, which seemed so singular when first induced in the laboratory and studied, is now known to play a large rôle in the ordinary manifestations of tuberculosis, syphilis and actinomycosis. It is true that vaccinia yields a vesicle distinguishable microscopically from that of smallpox. Yet all in all it can safely be said that the processes invoked by immunizations, vaccinations, and antisera are so natural to the body as to provoke few unique lesions, and these few negligible[1].

[1] Post-vaccinal encephalitis would seem to imply the introduction of a special disease entity. As yet it has not appeared in America.

(12)

Amongst the other so-called general diseases those of neoplastic character are remarkable in that, whilst knowing little of their intrinsic cause, we have in some instances greatly altered their pathology. It is not merely that one can remove large encapsulated tumours, freeing the host of a slavery to the growing tissue, that had made him a mere purveyor to it of food and water, like the white mouse with a growing implant. Radium and the Röntgen ray, agencies which produce peculiar and distinctive lesions in normal tissues, cause a special fate to overtake the neoplastic cells, one of colliquation and wholesale destruction. But cure has not yet been pushed so far as to prevent cancer deaths of the characteristic sort, with the old actions and reactions between growth and body, so far as one is as yet able to discern them.

Several other general diseases have been influenced in ways that change their manifestations radically, though the outcome in terms of the morbid cannot now be predicted. Only a little while ago patients with pernicious anaemia were kept alive by transfusing them, and the end sometimes became a choice between death from the original anaemia or from induced haemolysis of the

(13)

strange blood, this latter involving a new pathology in the sense in which the term is used in the present discussion. The event with patients saved now by liver extract, and free from cord lesions, is still problematic. Perhaps certain of them with blood kept in excellent state will succumb in ways unvisioned heretofore. And it is conceivable that diabetics preserved by insulin will eventually die of processes implicit in this malady but not encountered previously because life did not last sufficiently long. Insulin death as new pathology is very real. Nevertheless one has good reason to hope, from the effects of treating cretins with thyroid extract, that there are now no unperceived catastrophes in ambush for the diabetic.

Scrutinizing the consequences of cardiac and vascular disease, one sees nothing morbid that is new in spite of all present-day ameliorations. Surgeons can unite torn vessels as not before; and very, very occasionally the funnel of a mitral stenosis can be cut without inducing a circulatory *débâcle*. But the readjustments that ensue take place along the well-worn lines of pathological physiology. The modern treatments of nephritis and of heart disease, no matter how far pushed, yield no morphological novelties.

It would be possible to plod to the end of the list, emphasizing at every pause the fact that, though the aspects of disease have changed or been changed, though some new ills, mostly occupational, or already lurking, have come to the fore, the underlying actions and reactions within the body remain essentially what they were in the past. But it will be more summary to turn to a phase of medical activity, surgery, which should surely, one might think, have led to new responses on the part of the organism. And in one sense surgery has, in that these responses are new to the beholder, consisting as they do of frank reactions to situations brusquely created. But it is remarkable how many of these reactions have been encountered previously, as result of intercurrent situations not then understood. All that surgery has done in such instances is to make plain the relation of effect to cause, as for example in showing that tetany is due to insufficiency of the parathyroids, and myxoedema to a thyroid lack. The tendency on the part of the organism to play its game along the accustomed lines is so strong that the most radical of operative procedures seldom diverts it enduringly from this course. It is possible, of course, to attain

(15)

unwittingly to strange physiological consequences while proceeding toward cure. The loss of bile through the fistula that so often means safety after a gall-stone operation causes unique disturbances. But in general the adjustment for strange situations or defects arbitrarily and abruptly brought about is so rapid, adequate and subtle, has so little of the peculiar in it, that the surgeons themselves have been deceived until very recently into supposing that some organs really do not matter.

Turning now from the consequences of man's interference with disease, let us scrutinize the outcome of some of his ambitious efforts to alter the immemorial capabilities of the organism, and to provide it with fresh scope.

One of the means whereby improvement of the body has been sought—and one which testifies to great innocence of mind and an optimism justified by the event—has been by the removal of organs deemed unnecessary. Something has already been said on that score. The early recognition that the appendix is in truth a vestigial incumbrance led to other excisions, undertaken always as the lesser of two evils, that of having a potential or actual menace, and that of doing without something that had always been there. Now surgeons have come reluctantly to realize that nearly all that the body possesses it has an earnest, if undisclosed, need for. The practice of removing the normal gall bladder as "prophylaxis," when opportunity offers, is only now ceasing in certain parts of the United States. It has taken many case histories to prove that after loss of the organ the course of digestion does not run smooth. Even the removal of enlarged tonsils, such gratuitous apostles of iniquity as they seem, may be followed by a nodular hyperplasia of the lymphoid tissue of the throat,—a plain sign that they had performed a function, though what that function one can as yet only guess. At the moment we are realizing that illness is often referable to an interdependence amongst the ductless glands. It may be possible in the end to cure the manifest disease of one out of several such interacting organs (as *e.g.* exophthalmic goitre) by taking another organ out, just as the distortion of a paralysis involving the muscles on one side of a limb can be corrected by cutting those on the other, which pull it from shape. But not in this way will the potentialities of the human body be expanded. One is reminded of the sailor deprived of arms and legs by two successive cannon balls, who should have been saved, so Charles Lamb thought, as an ornament to society.

Yet the removal of diseased organs must be practised, willy-nilly; and a prime object of recent research has been to make up for lacks arising in this way or through the ravages of disease itself. Some organs that are mere chemical drudges can be wholly dispensed with, either at present or in the near future, because the principles that they furnish can be provided from without. This holds true now of the thyroids and para-thyroids, and doubtless soon will of the adrenals and pancreas. The substitution should create no new pathology except in so far as man fails in his duty to play night nurse and day nurse in compensation for the body lack, as when death results from too much or too little insulin. Chemicals we can supply; but there is no substitute for the ensconced, living elements which take up and destroy bacteria, or for those others that are made to clutch down upon the capillary channels, shutting them off at need. And it is already evident that the vast majority of organs play several rôles,

(18)

often indeed comprise an entire troupe in themselves, or, failing this, are controlled in a subtle, yet vital, way that cannot be artificially duplicated. After the liver has been taken out the loss of its immediate function in relation to carbohydrate metabolism can be readily compensated for, the life of the animal being markedly prolonged merely by injections of sugar; but death soon occurs, nevertheless, in the absence of the organ's other multifarious activities. The essential function of the lung in gas exchange is so simple, and carbon dioxide and oxygen ply so swiftly through thin, living membranes, that one might induce the formation of a vascular sponge which would serve, in respect to the gases, as artificial pulmonary tissue; but the control over this substitute which would enable the possessor of it to climb a flight of stairs would inevitably be missing. These are fantastic conceptions, but they have within them the truth that man's power to substitute for organs is so narrowly limited that the end may already be in sight.

It might be said that transplantation offers a way out. But those who know best the laws regulating this possibility think least of its scope. There was a time not far back when laboratory workers, having to recognize a perhaps exaggerated individuality in themselves and their fellows, could yet perceive but slight traces thereof in the smaller laboratory animals, least of all in the inbred albinos. One healthy white rat or rabbit seemed, so far as concerned visible responses, much the same as another, perhaps a little fatter or thinner, older, or sturdier, but that was all. Now we recognize what may be termed physical personalities in these creatures, personalities which, extending even to hardy tissues like the skin, involve these in disaster after transplantation. Consider for a moment the differences existing in the red cells of creatures of a single sort. In some species these differences are so marked that the individual can be recognized by means of them, as in Egyptian cattle. In others, rabbits for example, only rare traces of individuality are evident. Yet even in the case of rabbits it asserts itself when opportunity is given. One rabbit may so well utilize the blood of another, introduced in syringefuls day by day, that its red marrow, having no need to fabricate cells, will gradually cease to work, and the corpuscles proper to the animal will little by little diminish in number and disappear. Then in a night, almost, the body reacts against the foreign legions with a copious production of antibodies, killing off the corpuscles so fast that the marrow, caught all dismantled, cannot make up the loss in time to avert a well-nigh fatal anaemia. With other tissues, consisting of elements which are cells in the proper sense of the term, matters are even more difficult. Isotransplants of the thyroid of rabbits have been found to survive in only about one animal out of seventeen; and the event is precarious in the receptive host. There is the instance of a rabbit whose body appeared at first to be neutral soil since it tolerated and sustained thyroid grafts from six other individuals. Then the investigator introduced a transplant from a seventh, and this brought into play immunity processes which killed off not the new guest merely but the other six more or less desirable ones. Skin taken from one white mouse will scarcely ever grow on another though this other look like its twin. A dog kidney perfectly placed and vascularized in another dog, as shown by the fact that it functions, does so for but a brief while, then atrophies. Individuality has been too much for it. With the most miraculous of conceivable technics one cannot expect new stomachs for old until methods for the recognition of this individuality have been attained, and the compatible, unreluctant donor from amongst a crowd of the unsuited has been provided as well. The presence of a great need on the part of the organism makes matters no whit better. The creation of a lack by removal of a large part of a gland (thyroid, adrenal, spleen) appears to aid in the survival and functioning of grafts to the same animal of a part of the tissue removed. But if the grafts come from another host no such benefit accrues to them, and they die off. The intolerance of the organism has triumphed over its intense need. Though men can be separated into only four groups on the basis of manifest blood differences, there are others hidden in the bloods as shown by the differing immune bodies elicited when they are injected into rabbits. Individuality one cannot expect, nor should one hope, to conquer. When society has become duly informed and regimented it may be possible sometimes to choose successfully and to transplant complex organs; and in proportion as this becomes feasible some body lacks can be alleviated; but no new pathology will be created, save that of an unsought intolerance, already fairly known because

(22)

encountered in the laboratory and clinically illustrated by the results of transfusing incompatible blood.

Transplantation within the species, though so overwhelming a failure[1], is so for reasons that could not have been apprehended save by trial. One sees in it a splendid hope baulked. But the current attempts to transfer organs from one species to another have no such respectability, being, in the light of present knowledge, grotesque antics. A lion might well be trained to lie down with a lamb; but the normal body will always pounce upon strange tissue, and will pounce the harder the stranger the tissue is.

The substitution of tissues having proven impossible, for the present at least, it would seem that one might utilize small fragments of existing organs after excision of the diseased major part, perhaps stimulating these residua in new ways to hyperplasia or hypertrophy so that needs on the part of the body would be permanently supplied. But the cells of most of the highly specialized organs do not, apparently cannot, pro-

[1] The growth of transplanted tumour cells represents survival by aggression and hence stands without the general category.

liferate[1], though the response to the call upon them means life or death to the creature as a whole. And back of this obstacle, whatever its nature, there stands another in adult animals, that of reproducing the more or less complex structural arrangement which is essential to integrity and proper function. The difficulty is clearly seen in the case of such organ residua as are capable of responding to needs by an increase in size. When only half a kidney is left in an animal this suffices to support life, and while so doing it becomes larger, though not nearly reaching the original bulk, since no significant increase in the number of glomeruli and tubules occurs, the existing ones merely enlarging moderately and, in the case of the tubules, elongating. The lung tissue left by disease or operation does not sprout off new alveoli; the remaining ones merely get bigger. In the case of the liver, on the other hand, not only is the size of the organ reached once again by proliferation from a fragment, but the reconstitution is functionally perfect, new bile capillaries connecting up with the system already extant. Furthermore the

---

[1] Andrewes, Sir F. W., "Disease in the Light of Evolution," *Lancet*, 1926, ccx, 1075.

replacement is extremely swift. Through the study of delayed chloroform poisoning in the dog, which has cast so helpful a light upon the nature of this catastrophe in human beings and suggested a means to avert it, the fact has been ascertained that an entire half of the liver parenchyma, rendered necrotic by prolonged general anaesthesia of the animal, will be replaced within ten days, and so perfectly that not a trace of the injury remains. The dead cells in the lobular cords have been digested away, their places filled by proliferation of the survivors, and the healthy organ exists within its capsule as before. The same tendency to replacement is exerted effectually, though not as rapidly, when the parenchymal tissue has been removed instead of being destroyed *in situ*. Though only a quarter of it all be left the loss is made up, and one soon finds a liver of normal size. But the new organ is extraordinarily fragile. The return to the original bulk has been accomplished, not by a formation of new acini, but merely by a mushroom extension of the old, no adequate supporting framework having come into existence; and the result is that the eventual hepatic mass approximates to fresh, unshrunken blood clot in texture, and is nearly as liable to rupture. The substances which stimulate or further cell multiplication—and not a few have been turned up—are in general devoid of any effect to aid cell organization. The obstacle to successful reconstitution presented by the latter can be surmounted only where there are inherent, dormant potentialities, as in the case of some of the tissues of the cretin receiving thyroxin. But where these potentialities no longer exist—and the behaviour of the regenerating fragments of most complex organs gives no evidence of them—it would seem idle to expect help.

Though the ability of most organs for replacement is so unfortunately limited, there exists in many what would seem at first glimpse to be a profuse superfluity both of tissue and of functional capacity. Have not most people more brains than they use? Need one ask the question where youth, ever reluctant, is taught? One recalls William James' essay on the *Energies of Men*—those latent energies which are seldom put forth. Some of the material margins of safety, those of lung and kidney for example, have been disclosed more plainly by the encroachments of disease than by experiment, and have been known very long. The drastic

(26)

test of removal has shown that the liver is more than four times as large as immediate need requires, ten times indeed if it be helped a little in its rôle by the injection of sugar. Less than one-twentieth of the adrenal cortex will sustain the organism for a while. On necessary occasion as much as twenty feet of small intestine can be excised, and some of the subjects of the deprivation have appeared healthy throughout later years. Yet the excess of tissue and of functional ability is apparent only. Necessities lie back of its existence, not the necessities of a cribbed and cabined body, but those which arise out of the ordinary stresses of living, out of functional impacts. The condition of affairs becomes plain on study of an organ such as the liver which responds readily with hypertrophy or atrophy to changes in the general metabolic state, and has cells endowed with what is to all intents and purposes an inexhaustible capacity for hyperplasia. When three-fourths of the hepatic parenchyma is removed a regeneration of the remainder to the original size of the organ takes place, as has already been said, and to neither less nor more than this size unless the conditions of life which call for liver activity be altered. When this happens the size attained by the liver[1] will be found to vary *pari passu* with the demands upon the organ. The regeneration of the liver remnant in fasting animals restores the parenchyma to about half its original bulk only; but this small bulk is expressive of the existing functional needs, not of a lack of capacity to recover lost ground, as is plain from the circumstance that the intact liver of controls similarly fasted reaches the same small size within the same period of time by a process of atrophy. If one part of the liver of an animal living normally be placed at a disadvantage by diverting its rightful share of portal blood to the remainder, this remainder rapidly hypertrophies, and in proportion as it does so the tissue that was deprived insidiously dwindles and at length wholly disappears, despite the constant provision to it of blood by way of the hepatic artery, a provision that in the circumstances soon becomes superabundant. So far, so good. If, however, the hypertrophy be prevented from taking place, by ligating the bile duct which drains the region that would have been implicated in it, the

[1] Allowance must be made, of course, for blood content and for temporary deposits of glycogen, fat and protein.

(28)

atrophy elsewhere does not come about. There persists, under such circumstances, at least four times as much hepatic tissue as will suffice for immediate needs; yet no one can doubt that it does so to serve the organism. Size, in the absence of morbid change, is expressive of functional capacity. It follows that those organs which fail to increase in bulk after parts of them have been lopped off can be regarded as cripples. The twentieth of the adrenal cortex, which, as above mentioned, will suffice after the rest has been destroyed, eventually undergoes exhaustion atrophy because of the continued absence of hyperplasia, and death of the individual ensues.

So swift has been the testing out of the capabilities of the body by surgery that already, as the foregoing may have sufficiently indicated, a great deal is known of what can or cannot be expected of organs previously unapproachable. Surgical technique will always remain subject to change and improvement. Not so with the potentialities which the method exploits. One may expect these to be sharply demarcated within the next fifty years. Much of what has been learnt is disappointing; some ways are barred that had seemed most open. Not only are the reactions of the organism fixed in character, but this organism fails to lend itself easily to improvement, being predetermined for what it is to an extent that has only of late been reapprehended. But as against these limitations is the reaffirmation in highly material and fortunate ways of the old principle, that however brusquely the body be disturbed, nearly always the tide of vital activities sets in the direction of a normal standard, an ideal standard it might be termed, since it is one to which the individual himself may never at any time attain. The organism relieved or altered in surgical ways reverts so far as possible toward this standard, not to any new one. There are instances, it is true, in which it is thrust upon the horns of a physiological dilemma, as in the case of the vicious circles, so-called; but the situations of this sort which prove tolerable in a peremptory world are relatively few. So compelling is the tendency of the body to revert to the normal, and so effective are its methods, that although we now employ remedies of unexampled potency, and invoke repairs and readjustments with a success undreamt of in the past, there are few unhappy by-products in the form of novel morbid change.

This fact, at first sight surprising, is writ clear in the literature of pathological anatomy, a science first explored with proper tools not three human generations ago and become in much less time a familiar domain. In what important respects does the textbook on morbid anatomy of thirty years back differ from that of the present? Nearly all of the lesions common to man had been adequately recorded at the earlier date; and the great modern advances in the treatment of disease have found no reflection in bulky supplementary volumes dealing with new anatomical manifestations of what the body can do if it only has the chance. And this is not all. For morbid anatomy is merely the footprint left by physiology. One perceives through the essential connection between the two, in the light of what has just been said, that the range of responses within the body is limited, as further that the exigencies of the past have called most of said responses into play. The gaze of the modern physiologist or pathologist is directed, as was Virchow's, beyond the organs and tissues, which are the visible symbols of function, to the cells comprising them. And no law of the Medes was ever as fixed as those ruling the behaviour of the

(31)

cells, and no code has been as invariably sustained. One can be thankful that so little new pathology has developed, but not of the implication that the physiological resources of the body have so largely been tested out.

Ever since man first consciously realized his need for strength he has meddled with every accessible organ and system in the attempt to make these more capable in health, or to combat the encroachments of disease. A curious list could be drawn up of what these organs and systems have yielded. Some potentialities have been ably exploited by the body itself in the course of pathological change. What else is the cardiac hypertrophy in gradual compensation for circulatory ills, or the immense hyperplasia of parts of the liver that balances the destruction of parenchyma elsewhere in the *hepar lobatum* of syphilis? And when has man not tried to make himself into a prodigy of muscular power? Treatment by sweating must at least have been coeval with the acquisition of fire, if indeed it did not precede it with the use of furs. The realization that the gut has an inability to say "No" to substances presented to it for absorption doubtless came before mammoth steak did, and this peculiarity which is both its weakness and its strength has been played upon ever since. For purposes of mere comprehension no one has to be told by modern physiologists that the small intestine takes up the water presented to its surface whether there is a body need or not, the kidneys doing the rest. And there is no real cause for surprise in the observation that after transplantation of the ureters into the small intestine the wastes that the kidneys cast forth are so fully reabsorbed that death occurs from uraemia. But to possess a potentiality or an instrument, together with a variety of beliefs concerning how to use it, is quite another thing from wielding it with a purpose rendered single by knowledge. In these recent years for the first time nearly the whole body has been thrown open to man's attempts at improvement. And what has he done? He has had perforce to be content to juggle the old bag of tricks in new and artful ways. The exceptions do but point the rule.

There would have been no cause to emphasize these facts a hundred years ago. The potentialities of the human organism must then have seemed what they had always been; and what they must still seem to persons who rely on the identical healing forces that Aesculapius invoked. But many other forces do we now summon to aid us. And we are so dazzled and excited by the recent opportunity to comprehend a great deal very suddenly, so impressed with the strange engines, agencies, portents round about that we have come to entertain daring expectations of the body itself, the disclosure of activities as pervasive and influential as wireless waves. And such perhaps there will be; for man is now engaged, for the first time under favourable conditions, in a calculated exploitation of his own resources.

What can be expected of these? Anybody who has lived amidst a science during the last twenty years will have seen much happen that appeared incredible, and will be prepared for more. Yet it is a scientific curiosity that prompts one to try to answer the question just asked. Hints of the answer are to be found in the character of the daily tasks, and more especially of the emergencies, with which the various organs have had to cope during the development of the species. For the animal body carries no extra cylinders all set up for crises that have never yet come to pass. Viewed in the light of services to be rendered, those startling capabilities which find expression in artificially induced immunity to infectious disease startle no longer. For infections are menaces which increase by geometrical progression as the harmful micro-organisms divide; and to deal with them requires a mechanism even more expansible. The term "acquired immunity" means merely that the individual has strengthened or augmented his original resistance in the presence of specific infection[1]. No comparable mobilization of resources is required against other harmful extraneous agencies, for no other grows by such leaps and bounds. The body has evidently had in the past to fend against only very moderate extremes of heat and cold; and the demands upon it to endure variations in atmospheric pressure have been so slight that we are to all intents and purposes adapted for a plane world, not a cubic one, as the slow readjustment to high altitudes clearly attests. The most sudden and extreme of natural stresses, apart from those due to infection as above described, arise during the normal exigencies of work and play and the abnormal ones

[1] Smith, Theobald, "The Decline of Infectious Diseases in its Relation to Modern Medicine," *Journal of Preventive Medicine*, 1928, II, 345.

of accident and illness. The limits of these exigencies were narrowly set until this mechanized age, with its airplanes and caissons and stokeholes, brought unprecedented demands; and the capabilities of the body have not been enlarged to meet the new emergencies. When one scrutinizes the age-old influences of environment for what they may be worth in the way of capabilities as yet not drawn upon, it becomes evident that few genii can be expected to emerge from the ancient physiological bottle. The potentialities of the organs, known or inferred from the demands of the past, give ground for the belief that in the absence of mutations there will be no apotheosis of the body.

It is conceivable that with the help of pituitary extract or another substance a general increase in size may be achieved, such as would have been greatly welcomed in an age of brute strength. But now, as we more and more easily control our environment, this wanes in desirability. There may be not only an importance in being rather small—to adopt Professor Boycott's phrase[1]—but many pleasurable advantages.

[1] Boycott, A. E., "On the Sizes of Things, or the Importance of Being Rather Small," *Contributions to*

Certainly it is possible to be happy within our present dimensions. It is probable that humanity will be prepared by its other achievements to decline gigantism unless attended by a longer period of life in good health.

Does it follow from this rather dismal comment upon man's physical potentialities, comment warranted by the prevailing elation over what man has done, that most of his diseases, other than those now ordinarily termed preventable, are irrevocably saddled upon him? It is good to realize that this is not the case, save as concerns those ills which come upon the worn-out creature. To the infections man stands in a strategic relation that is worth going into because it is so curious. His enlightenment concerning them has not been the gradual outcome of thousands of years during which there might have developed types of infection fitted to survive intellectual perception. No, it has been abrupt and comprehensive. And in consequence the situation of the infections nowadays is not unlike that of the animal life in America when the settlers came. Nothing had prepared the birds and beasts

Medical and Biological Research, Dedicated to Sir William Osler, 1, 226, P. B. Hoeber, New York, 1919.

to survive the new weapons wielded by new hordes. Survive they did not. The contrast between the teeming life which Audubon[1] found in wild districts, and the desolation encountered by Thoreau[2] thirty years after, when these had been penetrated, tells the story clearly. The American brook trout, mettlesome though he is, is still a fool, where he exists at all. There has not been opportunity as yet for the least foolish amongst the survivors to give rise to a really clever breed. But the British brown trout has adroitly been fished for hundreds of years. He knows his world quite well. One sees him poised, calm, adequate, immense, under the bridge that spans the clear little thread of water in the public garden at Winchester. He has come up from the river and is well aware of what he is about. It is not for nothing that his ancestors have existed for a vast number of trouty generations in a state of symbiosis with the British Empire—of a somewhat tempered symbiosis, it is true, on the part of the Empire.

[1] Audubon, J. J., *Delineations of American Scenery and Character*, with an Introduction by Francis Hobart Herrick, G. A. Baker and Co., New York, 1926.

[2] Thoreau, H. D., *The Maine Woods*, 1863.

The adaptations whereby infections persist have evolved out of association with man as a being that does not think. His creature senses they can elude, even his mechanical aids to such senses, as in the case of the filterable viruses; and they or their vectors can cope with an animal cunning. The yellow fever mosquito advances indirectly from behind the door as one sits on the sill in the cool of the evening; and it does not alight upon the top of the hand, but under the elbow. That its conduct is due simply to a preference for shade does not lessen its success. A knowledge of the menace and its habits, though, combined with some oiling and wire-screening, and it is done for. The carefully built up cycles whereby the animal parasites are passed on and perpetuated become just so many shattered, preposterous schemes, once they are clear to view. It is not through superior adaptations that malaria, trypanosomiasis, and yellow jack hold such large portions of the earth, but because of the condition of the tropics and some lack still of complete understanding. Yet we are none too soon in devastating the infections. The histories of tuberculosis and of syphilis show how man's inherent weaknesses of character can

(39)

be utilized for the spread and perpetuation of disease[1].

Which of man's other major ills are adventitious in the sense that the infections are? The patient says, "I have a cold," not "I am a cold," though he frequently feels as if he were. And granting that what he says merely expresses the old idea of possession, one is certain, nevertheless, that his statement is correct. But how about "I have cancer"? Should it not be, "I am cancer"? To the morbid anatomist at least, this would appear more nearly true. But not to the student of cancer in animals, even though he is unable to say what the cause of the disease is. For he finds that merely by putting tar week after week on the backs of male white mice, animals in which malignant growths are excessively rare, he can make cancers appear where none ever grow ordinarily, and this not in an occasional animal but in practically all. The extraneous influence, the tar, has made the difference between cancer and no cancer. The closer the disease in human beings is scrutinized, the more does it appear to be the direct outcome of injuries or functional perver-

[1] Krause, A., "Tuberculosis and the Public Health," *American Review of Tuberculosis*, 1928, XVIII, 271.

sions which are often completely negligible save in this consequence of them. One cannot but conclude that cancer is foisted upon the human fabric out of which it is built.

When one takes up the other important diseases which cut man off before age is upon him, grouping together those which are, at least in the theoretical sense, extraneous, a significant fact emerges, namely this, that in direct proportion as a malady is understood does it come to appear avoidable, or if not avoidable, remediable. Of all the ills that flesh is heir to, few indeed does it inherit by right, if one assumes, as the facts allow, that the cerebrum with its workings is a part of said flesh. There are numerous, but fortunately minor, exceptions. No one save the eugenist will contest the status as such of hemophilia or congenital heart disease, hernias or polydactilism. But can one venture to say nowadays of even such a riddle as "poor man's gout" that it is inherent in the human frame? During the War, when the Germans could not get meat, they were freed from attacks of gout. And what of gastric ulcer, of biliary calculi, of exophthalmic goitre? There is no need to go through the entire category of ills, yet one may pause a moment at diabetes. For the recent recognition that the disease is largely the penalty of obesity and other controllable states has shoved it over into the category of extraneous maladies, so far as concerns many cases; while irrespective of this a remedy has been found which is applicable even to those instances which are based, so one still has to think, on constitutional defect. The mind has helped the body so well that the question of whether the latter has inherited its misfortune or brought it upon itself becomes subsidiary. So too it is with pernicious anaemia, with certain types of goitre and many other ills of derivation still doubtful.

To practical men the foregoing discussion of whether a given disease is extraneous or intrinsic in nature may seem a mere flourishing about on paper. Certain maladies that are wholly preventable in the abstract are unavoidable in real deed; for though they can be thought of merely as occupational diseases, unfortunately the occupation is that of existing as a human creature, only too often one with constitutional liabilities and idiosyncracies. The individual man does not, cannot, live in a shell closed off from streptococci. And how is he to prevent those little, unseen injuries upon which

(42)

cancer arises in the viscera? There are infectious agents cleaving so closely to him, as for example *Staphylococcus aureus*, that he will always have to combat their attacks, for abolished they cannot be. And there are still other micro-organisms living peacefully in or alongside him that may come to rend him suddenly through chance changes in their own abilities[1]. Furthermore, through infirmities of will or judgment, not a few disorders that are theoretically avoidable will long continue to be brought upon bodies that have not earned them. In a dialogue after the antique manner between the mind and the body, in which they contest their virtues, the body could urge that it acts more immediately and directly in emergencies, is more self reliant, does not hesitate between alternatives, is fertile in resource and readjustment, and is infinitely, infinitely, the more persevering. It could say, rather bitterly, that given a co-operation of equal vigour on the part of the mind, and they would have begun to live far more successfully together.

Not only do mind and body have to dwell in a companionship that is too often against the best interests of either, but there are

[1] Theobald Smith, *loc. cit.*

other minds all about interfering with them both. The seriousness of this implication has yet to come home to the hygienist, flushed as he is with material triumphs. He has even been heard to say when speaking of men as a race, that they will gain mastery over mind and spirit, and thus prevent disease. Is it perhaps the hygienist's statistical fodder that causes him to think thus in terms of that *isocephaly*, that placing of the heads all at one level, no matter where they belong, which renders the pictured bands of the Greek vases so pleasing? William James was nearer the truth in his recognition of two enduring classes of humanity, the mystics and the rationalists. For the mystics, as James says, two and two make, not four but some other number; and they hold the rationalist, who is sure he adds correctly, in a detestation which is amply returned. Not a few of them would come away from the sight of a consolidated lung at autopsy, still believing it to be the product of evil thoughts. The militant mystic, a conscientious objector to established fact, will always strive against rational medicine.

These varied impediments of mind and circumstance, while disheartening to the practitioner, do not in any way weaken the concept that most maladies are, in the last analysis, avoidable. And this concept confers upon practical workers all the benefits of an ideal.

One does not have to compare individually the great causes of death fifty years ago with those of the present in order to realize that they are not the same. But there is a drab implication in the change, since in it one sees humanity marching up close to the ultimate barrier of age. The major decreases in the mortality of civilized countries have been in tuberculosis, diphtheria, typhoid, scarlet fever, and the diarrhoea of infants[1]— how barbarous the epoch already seems as the names are told off! Now men succumb principally to heart disease, nephritis, apoplexy, cancer and pneumonia[1],—a sobering list for any optimist. Let it be granted that pneumonia will go, that cancer will be cured, with or without understanding it, that much heart disease and nephritis will be avoided or alleviated, what then? The physician then must cope with the old body, indeed he is already coping. And in this body,

[1] Winslow, C. E. A., in *Whither Mankind, A Panorama of Modern Civilization*. Edited by Charles Beard, Longmans, Green and Co., New York, 1928.

ageing irregularly but surely, first this system and then that, one process of involution hastening another, he finds a paradox. Little by little as life has been lived, not the organism alone, but the very cells comprising it have turned away from the standard of the normal so stoutly maintained heretofore. Whereas previously the swing of events had been always in the direction of health, however rude the disturbance, now even in the absence of disease or interference the trend is to the pathological. At the present day the changes proper, or one might better say inevitable, to old age have not been nearly disentangled from those of avoidable wear and tear. The share of heredity in senile processes has been no more than touched upon. But the phenomena which are assuredly referable to ageing as such[1], the atrophies, fibroses, pigmentations, metaplasias, hyperkeratoses, the renunciations of function—as in fat cells which no longer store fat—all these show that a changed and still changing fabric exists, one with a standard of health that diverges from the ordinary, a health dubiously supported in the very midst of

[1] Warthin, A. S., *Old Age, The Major Involution*, P. B. Hoeber and Co., New York, 1929.

retrogression. The responses to abnormal situations are also different. When the need to hypertrophy meets the tendency to senile atrophy, what then? The answer only too frequently is, disaster. Senility has the right of way. The physician must of necessity interfere to stop it; and some of his attempts upon a fabric that is already unstable, in which there no longer exists a profound impulse to revert to the normal, cannot but have extraordinary consequences. The situation now coming upon mankind as a sort of cumulative emergency, that of having to keep old bodies fit, of urging them out of bad situations, will produce a new Dance of Death. A new one in the quantitative sense there already is. The individuals who are now conserved throughout adult life die of diseases that have waited upon age from time immemorial but that have had few targets in the past, not hosts of them as now. And qualitatively too the dance must alter somewhat. Yet at this present moment in world affairs, when everywhere there is stirring and advancing, prying and comprehending, mastering and bettering, it is perhaps well to realize that the accustomed responses of our own bodies have resisted modernization. In the brief

(47)

period since Linacre's day the Dance of Death has lengthened, the music has turned sweeter, Death has become less boorish, his partner not so passive, but the measure is still the same, still the only one that the human organism has proved able to tread.

There is a part of the future so implicit in the present that one can think of both together, and, indulging in a favourite pursuit of the exact scientist, extrapolation, trace events beyond the rim of the actual.

One can perceive that in not so very long as time goes, the loud hymns of the physiologists in praise of the body will have died away. The limitations of capability and duration of that compact entity will have become so known as to be irksome. And gradually as this happens the search for an elixir of life will be resumed more avidly than ever. Unless mutations occur to alter the human frame people will have become like garden strawberries, carefully tended to a perfection still so vulnerable to circumstance that they can easily revert to the old flawed condition, as garden strawberries do when let run wild amid weeds. Mutations are man's best hope, to save the situation disclosed by the mortality tables which show that all our civilization has not extended the ultimate limit of life the least fraction of a year.

One sees the child of a future that is just a little way up the hill as brought into an existence largely safeguarded for him, but in which society will expect him to do somewhat more for others than now and vastly more for himself, in order to protect his body from what will be deemed a premature deterioration. In retrospect our existence may come to seem reckless and care free. Yet already life has become to no inconsiderable extent a system of ordered avoidances. The requests not to spit, not to cough, not to sneeze, become daily more imperative. And there are omens most serious in the introduction of habits which do not so plainly hinge on the need to avoid a peril. The recent dissemination of tooth brushes amongst the masses is an instance in point. Anyone with his wits about him, who is near the tap, can use a tooth brush without calling upon fortitude. But it will be different when one must not obey the old animal urges, when youth is asked to go softly, to avoid living ardently and exhaustingly, in order to save heart and kidneys for an old age which is scarcely apprehended, much less relished in thought. Yet that is the inevitable trend of the times. It has become clear to layman as well as doctor that not only do the ways of the wicked eventually perish with highly concrete and unpleasant physical accompaniments, but that so too if more insidiously do those of the hasty, of the irritable, of the too energetic, of the careless, of those who lack persistence, and even, alas, of those who are softly generous or unwarrantably optimistic. We have now advanced to a state in which anything perceptibly affecting physical or moral health is reprobated. A little time and it will take its place amongst the vices. Those who do not handle themselves wisely in all physical and mental respects will be considered wasters, and insensibly the phrase "He had no one to blame but himself" will turn to "He was a bad fellow." With the growth of this mental attitude, and of the average length of life, the question will no longer seem so vivid of whether it is preferable to write poetry and die at thirty, or prose and live to eighty. The choice is not an inevitable one even now.

Long after man has conquered nature in general he will still be struggling with human nature, learning to live at the best of terms with it. The noxious influences of the extraneous he can eliminate; himself, with his formidable capabilities for self-mutilation, he carries along the way. Were the way merely one of expediency, of tending upon protoplasm and nuclei for their last possible yield, the journey would be dire, a shuffling, hang-dog progress. But with the body cared for, the mind can play in the sun. And the new science of living long and well will bring with it a science of dying, to supplement that most difficult of arts.